MYRA ROWSE

Charming
COUNTRY
Fall

COLORING BOOK
FOR ADULTS

A sincere thank you for choosing our coloring book.

Discover a world of inspiration for coloring these pages! Stay updated with news about our latest books and exciting promotions by following us on Facebook and Instagram:
https://www.facebook.com/MyraRowseColoringBooks
https://www.instagram.com/myrarowsecoloringbooks

Before you start, take a moment to try your coloring tools on the test pages at the end. If you wish to use markers or other wet mediums, please place a thick sheet of paper under the page you are working on to prevent any bleed-through.
Happy coloring!

With love
Myra
ROWSE

This coloring
book belongs to:

_____

_____

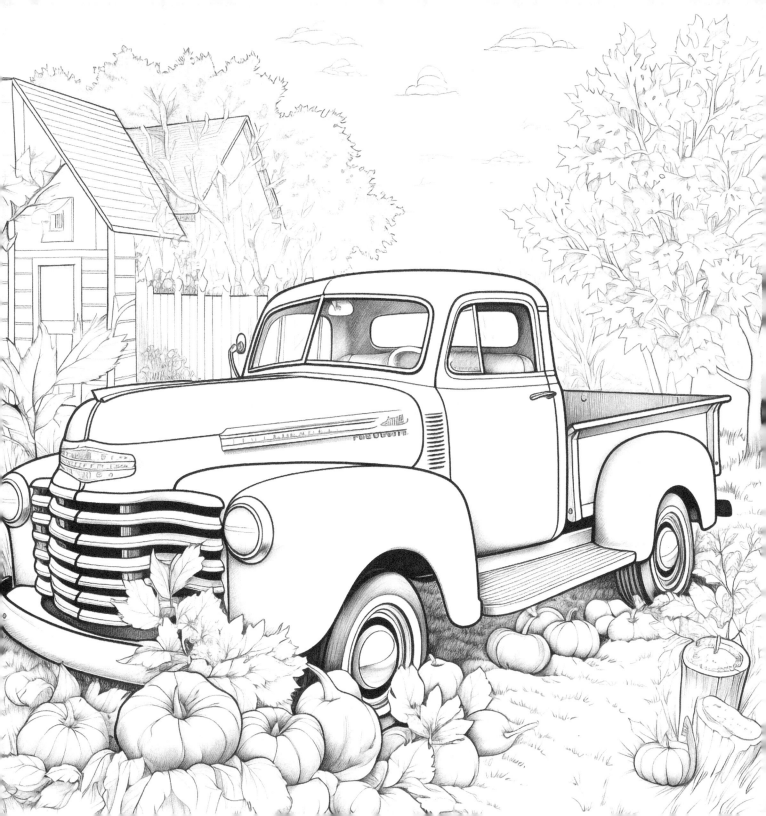

Thank You!

As the author of this coloring book, I wanted to take a moment to express my heartfelt gratitude for choosing our book and completing this incredible journey. We understand that life can be stressful, and that's why we're committed to creating coloring books that inspire and offer hours of artistic enjoyment and stress relief. As a small, family-owned company, we take great pride in knowing that our books have brought joy and comfort to your life. We appreciate your support and are grateful to be a part of your creative adventure.
If you enjoyed this book and found it to be a source of joy, relaxation, and growth, we kindly invite you to leave a review on Amazon. Your words carry immense power and can make a significant impact on our small business. Your support will not only help us reach more customers but also inspire us to continue creating wonderful books.
You can find our books on amazon by searching for Myra Rowse or by going to our author page link:
https://www.amazon.com/author/myra-rowse

With deep appreciation,

Myra ROWSE

COLOR TEST PAGE

COLOR TEST PAGE

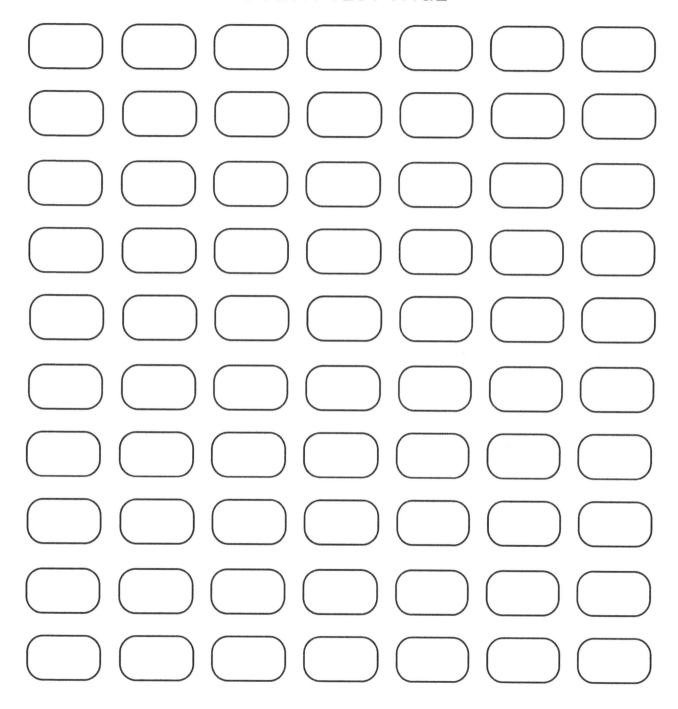

ABOUT THE AUTHOR

"Unique, beautifully designed coloring books for a joyful life"
is not just a tagline for Myra; it's a mission.
Meet Myra Rowse, the creative force behind a kaleidoscope of joy in the world of adult coloring. With a rich artistic background, Myra combines her passion for art with innovative techniques to create a brand that's as unique as it is delightful.
In the vibrant realm of coloring books, Myra's creations begin with images inspired by her own artistic vision and created with the help of AI. These designs are then carefully reviewed, redrawn where needed and enhanced digitally, blending cutting-edge technology with her artistic expertise. This thoughtful fusion ensures a high-quality and enjoyable coloring experience. Myra's books feature a wide variety of themes, ensuring there's something for everyone to enjoy. Whether you're a coloring novice or a seasoned pro, each page is an open canvas where the only rule is to have fun and relax. Myra believes there's no wrong way to color – it's all about expressing yourself freely, regardless of your artistic background.
So, dive into Myra's world, pick up your favorite coloring tools, and let the colors of joy and self-discovery fill the pages of your own unique masterpiece.
Don't forget to tag your progress and finished art with
#MyraRowseColoringBooks on Instagram and Facebook!

Myra
ROWSE

Made in the USA
Monee, IL
18 October 2024

68225854R00063